Rediscover Your Story:
A Journal for Creative Exploration

Drew Kimble

ISBN: 1978008945
ISBN-13: 978-1978008946

INTRODUCTION

This is not your typical writing journal, but a creative tool that can help you reconnect with yourself and rediscover your story.

As much as I enjoy creative writing prompts and daily free-writing as a way to get the imagination going first thing in the morning, I think we sometimes forget about the importance of self-reflection.

Don't get me wrong, being creative and firing up your imagination is awesome, but so is taking a moment in your busy day to better understand who you are and what you are capable of becoming.

It's kind of like deciding to go for a walk rather than a run.

Many of us use running as a way to push ourselves both physically and mentally. Walking, on the other hand, is often a much slower and reflective type of activity. This doesn't mean that one is better than the other. In fact, both of these activities should probably have a place in our daily life because they complement one another and serve different purposes.

The same holds true for writing journals such as this. There is a time for creative writing prompts and there's a time for the reflective writing prompts that you'll find in this journal. Some of these prompts will make you laugh, and some will make you think, while others will dare you to reimagine your future.

Private and public writing

In this age of blogs, emails, and endless social media updates, I think many of us are doing a lot more "public" writing, which is where we write something that is intended to be read by others. What seems to be lacking, however, is the more private contemplative type of writing that may only have an audience of one.

This type of writing is not about trying to impress others with our status updates and accomplishments. Instead, it gives us the opportunity to dig a little deeper and perhaps rediscover something meaningful we may have forgotten along the way.

Now having said that, this journey won't always be filled with rainbows and unicorns. Digging through our personal treasure trove of memories can often be an unpredictable and emotional minefield, but it is still a journey worth taking.

Handwriting vs. Typing

We've become a culture of online skimmers and clickers.

The physical act of writing on paper is something that requires us to slow down and focus, instead of multitasking on our laptops where we are always just a click away from checking our email or watching hilarious cat videos on YouTube.

Writing in a paper journal can also provide us with a sense of permanence that is often lacking in our transient digital world.

Unlike a Facebook status update, a paper journal like this can create an enduring snapshot of who you were at this moment for you to rediscover down the road.

This is also the reason why I created this journal as a physical book that you can carry with you almost anywhere.

Take it with you to work, the park, the dentist office, or anywhere else you may have the chance to write for 10 minutes. Instead of mindlessly grabbing your phone or tablet to fill these idle moments, use it as an opportunity to dig deeper and rediscover your story.

How to use this journal

As I've mentioned in my previous books, creativity is usually the result of self-discipline and habit rather than a random gift from the gods. This is why it's important to make writing a daily part of your life even if you may only have a few minutes to sit down and put some words to paper.

As far as the writing prompts themselves, some people like to go in order, but you don't have to. Others, like myself, may prefer to pick a random page each day. Either way, if you're not interested in a specific prompt, feel free to choose a different one.

Group activity

Finally, just because a journal like this can become deeply personal, that doesn't necessarily mean you can't share this adventure with someone else.

In fact, I would encourage you to invite your spouse, best friend, or family members to join you on this creative journey. All you have to do is pick a writing prompt, set a timer for 10-15 minutes, and then share your results (or not) with the group.

Like my other books, I created this writing journal because it was something that I needed to have in my own life. I hope that it will enrich yours as well.

"SELF-REFLECTION IS THE SCHOOL OF WISDOM."

—BALTASAR GRACIAN

.

THERE WAS
ANOTHER LIFE
THAT I MIGHT
HAVE HAD,
BUT I AM HAVING
THIS ONE
-KAZUO ISHIGURO

FIRST THINGS...

FIRST SONG YOU REMEMBER HEARING:

FIRST PET:

FIRST CAR:

FIRST "R" RATED MOVIE:

FIRST DATE:

FIRST CONCERT:

FIRST CRUSH:

FIRST FRIEND:

FIRST THING YOU BOUGHT WITH OWN MONEY:

FIRST BOYFRIEND/GIRLFRIEND:

FIRST TEACHER:

FIRST KISS:

FIRST JOB:

FIRST FOREIGN COUNTRY VISITED:

FIRST TIME YOU FELT LIKE AN ADULT:

CAN ANYTHING
BE SADDER THAN WORK
LEFT UNFINISHED?
YES, WORK NEVER BEGUN.
-CHRISTINA ROSSETTI

LIST 5 THINGS THAT SOMEONE WHO HAS JUST MET YOU FOR THE FIRST TIME WOULD MOST LIKELY SAY ABOUT YOU:

1.)

2.)

3.)

4.)

5.)

WHAT'S ONE THING YOU WISH THEY WOULD MENTION, BUT PROBABLY WOULDN'T?

IF EVERYTHING
IS UNDER
CONTROL,
YOU ARE
GOING
TOO SLOW.
-MARIO ANDRETTI

WHAT IS SOMETHING ABOUT YOUR PAST YOU FREQUENTLY LIE TO PEOPLE ABOUT?

LIFE IS CHANGE.
GROWTH IS OPTIONAL.
CHOOSE WISELY
-KAREN KAISER CLARK

PUT A STAR WHERE YOU THINK YOU ARE ON THE FOLLOWING SPECTRUMS:

PATIENT --- IMPATIENT

AGGRESSIVE --- PASSIVE

OPEN -- CLOSED

GIVING -- TAKING

LISTENER -- TALKER

GENEROUS -- FEARFUL

PESSIMISTIC -- OPTIMISTIC

ARRIVE EARLY ------------------------------------ ARRIVE LATE

PLANNER --SPONTANEOUS

FLEXIBLE --- STUBBORN

SOCIAL --- LONER

TAKING CHANCES ---------------------------------TAKING IT EASY

I DON'T WANT
TO DISCOUNT
TALENT
AND ABILITY,
BUT I STILL
MAINTAIN THAT
A LOT
OF IT
IS JUST SHEER
DESIRE.
-DON HENLEY

DESCRIBE 3 WAYS YOU ARE DIFFERENT THIS YEAR THAN LAST.

NOW, DESCRIBE 3 WAYS YOU PLAN TO BE DIFFERENT NEXT YEAR.

THERE IS NEITHER
PAINTING,
NOR SCULPTURE,
NOR MUSIC,
NOR POETRY.
THE ONLY TRUTH
IS CREATION.
-UMBERTO BOCCIONI

LIST 7 SONGS THAT WOULD MAKE UP THE MIXTAPE OF YOUR LIFE SO FAR:

1.)

2.)

3.)

4.)

5.)

6.)

7.)

BONUS POINTS: NAME THE SONG THAT BEST DESCRIBES YOUR UPCOMING YEAR.

WHAT IS SOMETHING YOU OFTEN DO THAT PUSHES PEOPLE AWAY?

HOW OFTEN DO YOU USE THIS ABILITY AND WHY?

If somebody's
trying
to shut you up,
sing louder
and,
if possible,
better.
-Salman Rushdie

WHAT IS YOUR FAVORITE NOVEL? WHEN DID YOU FIRST READ IT,
AND WHAT WAS IT ABOUT THE BOOK THAT MADE IT YOUR FAVORITE?

BONUS POINTS: LEAVE A COPY OF THIS NOVEL FOR SOMEONE ELSE IN A PUBLIC PLACE. ON THE INSIDE COVER WRITE: *"THIS IS MY FAVORITE BOOK. I HOPE YOU ENJOY IT!"* AND THEN SIGN YOUR NAME.

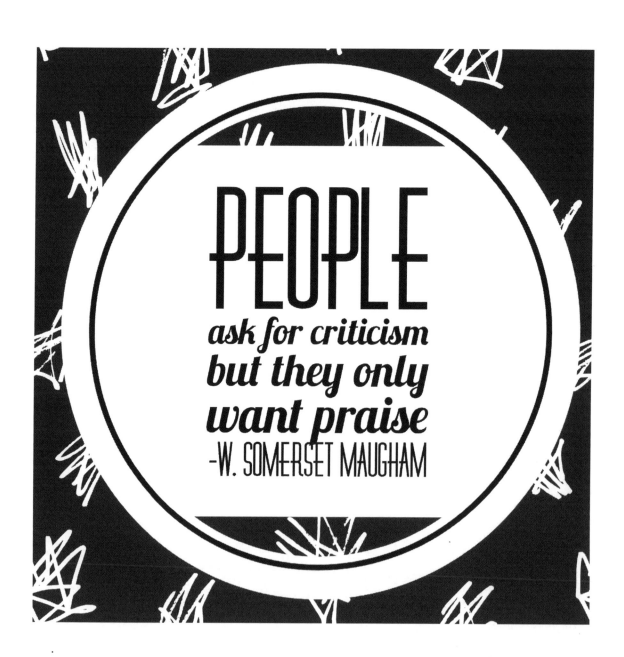

USE 3 WORDS TO DESCRIBE...

YOUR MOM:

YOUR DAD:

YOUR CHILDHOOD HOME:

YOUR BROTHER:

YOUR SISTER:

YOUR BEST FRIEND:

YOUR HIGH SCHOOL EXPERIENCE:

YOUR 16-YEAR-OLD SELF:

YOUR SIGNIFICANT OTHER:

THE LAST YEAR:

YOUR CURRENT SELF:

YOUR FUTURE SELF:

great THINGS ARE
DONE BY A SERIES
of small things BROUGHT TOGETHER
—ViNCENT VAN GOGh

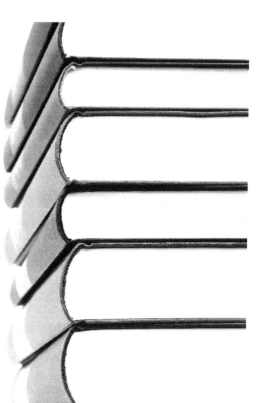

WHAT IS ONE HABIT YOU WOULD LIKE TO GET RID OF THIS YEAR?

WHAT NEW HABIT WOULD YOU LIKE TO PICK UP THIS YEAR?

CREATIVITY TAKES

COURAGE.

- HENRI MATISSE

WHAT ARE 5 THINGS YOU WOULD LIKE TO GO BACK AND SAY TO YOUR 12-YEAR-OLD SELF?

1.)

2.)

3.)

4.)

5.)

DON'T TRY TO BE DIFFERENT. JUST BE GOOD. TO BE GOOD IS DIFFERENT ENOUGH

• • •

Arthur Freed

THINGS THAT GIVE ME ENERGY…

THINGS THAT TAKE MORE ENERGY THAN THEY ARE WORTH…

LIST 3 BOOKS YOU WOULD LIKE TO READ THIS YEAR:

1.)

2.)

3.)

WHY DID YOU CHOOSE THESE PARTICULAR BOOKS?

NOTHING IS A
WASTE OF
TIME IF
YOU USE THE
EXPERIENCE
WISELY
-AUGUSTE RODIN

DESCRIBE WHAT YOU HAD HANGING ON THE WALLS OF YOUR CHILDHOOD BEDROOM.

WHICH OF THESE ITEMS WERE YOU THE PROUDEST OF?

WHICH OF THESE ITEMS ARE YOU THE MOST EMBARRASSED BY NOW?

SOMETIMES
AN ARTIST'S
FIRST INVENTION
IS HERSELF
-STEPHANIE VAUGHN

LIST 5 THINGS YOU HAVE DONE BUT WOULD <u>NOT</u> DO AGAIN:

1.)

2.)

3.)

4.)

5.)

LIST 5 THINGS YOU WOULD LIKE TO DO BUT HAVEN'T YET:

1.)

2.)

3.)

4.)

5.)

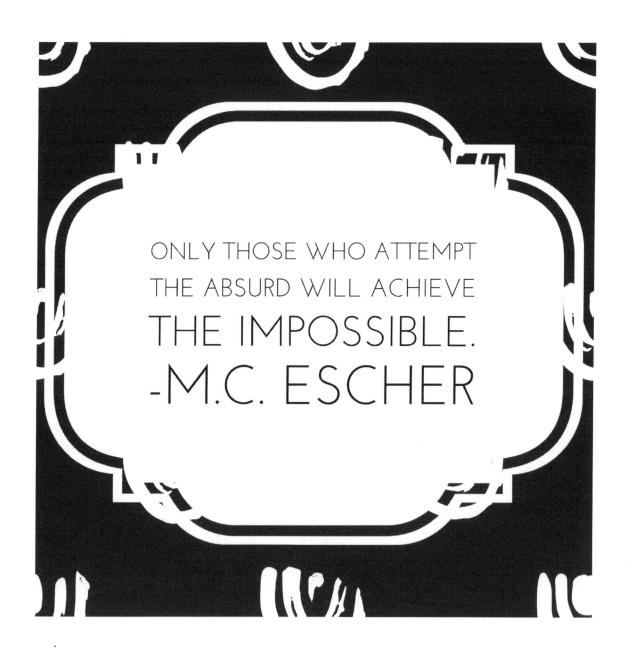

ONLY THOSE WHO ATTEMPT
THE ABSURD WILL ACHIEVE
THE IMPOSSIBLE.
-M.C. ESCHER

LIFE INVENTORY

(CIRCLE ALL THAT APPLY)

I HAVE...

DRIVEN A MOTORCYCLE   VISITED A FOREIGN COUNTRY

JUMPED OFF THE HIGH DIVE   SNOOPED ON SOMEONE ELSE'S PHONE

RECEIVED A TROPHY   SHOT A GUN   GOT INTO A FIST FIGHT

MET SOMEONE FAMOUS   CHEATED ON MY PARTNER

GOTTEN A MASSAGE   SAVED SOMEONE'S LIFE   BEEN TO A STRIP CLUB

HAD COSMETIC SURGERY   LEARNED A FOREIGN LANGUAGE

PASSED OUT DRUNK   GIVEN A TOAST   GIVEN A EULOGY

STAYED UP ALL NIGHT   BROKEN SOMEONE'S HEART

LEARNED A CARD TRICK   ATTENDED A CLASS REUNION   BEEN ON TV

SANG KARAOKE   FAKED AN ORGASM   WRITTEN A POEM

LEARNED CPR   LEARNED HOW TO WHISTLE

DELETED MY INTERNET HISTORY   LIED TO MY BOSS   ADOPTED A PET

COMPLETED A 10K RACE   CLIMBED A MOUNTAIN

CHANGED THE OIL IN MY CAR   STALKED AN OLD LOVER ONLINE

TO BE TRULY CREATIVE, YOU HAVE TO WORK BEYOND WHAT YOU KNOW

-JOHN FERRIE

WHAT IS THE KINDEST THING YOU'VE DONE THAT NO ONE ELSE KNOWS ABOUT?

WHAT IS THE WORST THING YOU'VE DONE THAT NO ONE ELSE KNOWS ABOUT?

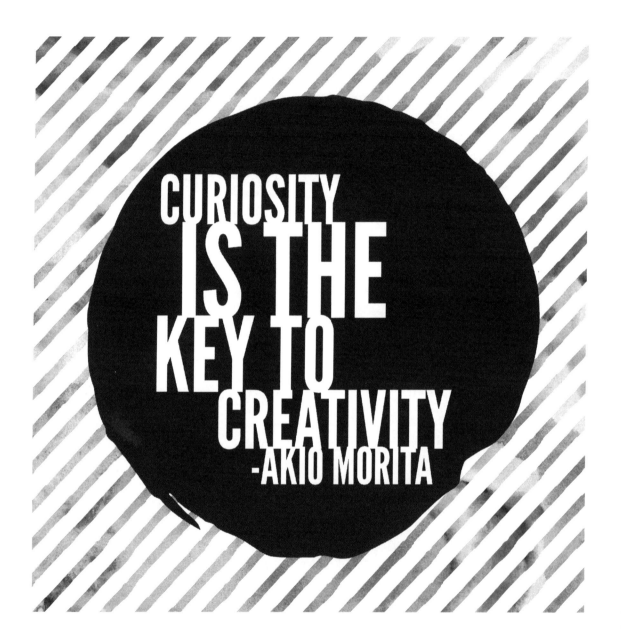

CURIOSITY
IS THE
KEY TO
CREATIVITY
-AKIO MORITA

WHAT ARE YOUR 5 FAVORITE FOODS?

1.)

2.)

3.)

4.)

5.)

WHAT ARE 3 FOODS YOU SHOULD LIKE BUT DON'T?

1.)

2.)

3.)

WHAT ARE 3 FOODS YOU SHOULDN'T LIKE BUT DO?

1.)

2.)

3.)

DON'T JUDGE EACH DAY BY THE *harvest you reap* BUT BY THE SEEDS THAT *you plant* -ROBERT LOUIS STEVENSON

THIS OR THAT?

(CIRCLE YOUR PREFERENCE)

CAT or DOG   SWEET or SALTY   WINE or BEER

OPTIMIST or PESSIMIST   LOGIC or INTUITION   CONCERT or PLAY

COFFEE or TEA   DREAMER or REALIST   BOLD or SUBTLE

MOVIE or BOOK   CAMPING or HOTEL   PEPSI or COKE

TEXTING or TALKING   BEAUTY or BRAINS   ART or SCIENCE

SPRING or FALL   THE JOURNEY or THE DESTINATION

GOING OUT or STAYING IN   TRUTH or DARE   CHROME or FIREFOX

POWERFUL or HAPPY   SPOTIFY or PANDORA   BEACH or MOUNTAINS

EXPLORE or RELAX   FRUITS or VEGETABLES   DRIVE or RIDE

LOUD or QUIET   CREMATION or BURIAL   MAC or WINDOWS

BEING A PART OF SOMETHING or BEING INDEPENDENT

CARNIVORE or VEGETARIAN   CITY or OPEN SPACE   WEALTH or FAME

THE TRAGEDY **OF LIFE** IS NOT THAT IT ENDS SO SOON,

BUT THAT WE WAIT SO LONG TO BEGIN IT.
-W. M. LEWIS

FINISH THESE SENTENCES

WORK IS...

FAMILY IS...

SUCCESS IS...

MONEY IS...

LOVE IS...

HAPPINESS IS...

REGRET IS...

YOU DON'T HAVE TO SAY EVERYTHING TO SAY SOMETHING.

— Beth Moore —

WHAT IS THE HARDEST LESSON THAT YOU EVER HAD TO LEARN?

HOW HAS YOUR LIFE CHANGED BECAUSE OF IT?

EXPLORE. DREAM. DISCOVER.

-MARK TWAIN

LIST THE 5 MOST IMPORTANT TRAITS THAT YOU LOOK FOR IN A POTENTIAL PARTNER:

1.)

2.)

3.)

4.)

5.)

WHAT ARE 5 TRAITS THAT YOU BRING TO A POTENTIAL RELATIONSHIP?

1.)

2.)

3.)

4.)

5.)

I MYSELF AM MADE
ENTIRELY OF FLAWS,
STITCHED TOGETHER
WITH GOOD INTENTIONS.
-AUGUSTEN BURROUGHS

WHAT DO YOU THINK YOU SHOULD STOP WORRYING SO MUCH ABOUT?

WHAT DO YOU THINK YOU SHOULD POSSIBLY WORRY ABOUT MORE?

IT IS NEVER TOO LATE TO BE WHAT YOU MIGHT HAVE BEEN
-GEORGE ELIOT

THINK OF SOMEONE YOU WOULD LIKE TO ASK FOR THEIR ADVICE.
COME UP WITH 5 QUESTIONS YOU WOULD LIKE THEM TO ANSWER:

1.)

2.)

3.)

4.)

5.)

BONUS POINTS: IF THEY ARE STILL ALIVE, WRITE THEM AN EMAIL (YOU NEVER KNOW!)

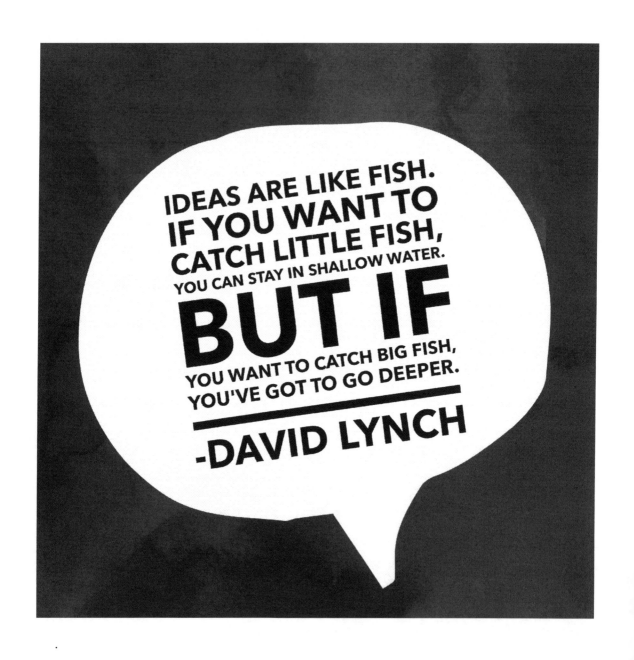

ON A SCALE OF 1-10, HOW DO YOU THINK YOUR 12-YEAR-OLD SELF WOULD RATE YOUR CURRENT LIFE IN THE FOLLOWING AREAS . . .

YOUR JOB: 1——2——3——4——5——6——7——8——9——10

YOUR ROMANTIC SITUATION: 1——2——3——4——5——6——7——8——9——10

THE CAR YOU DRIVE: 1——2——3——4——5——6——7——8——9——10

YOUR SOCIAL LIFE: 1——2——3——4——5——6——7——8——9——10

THE PLACE YOU LIVE: 1——2——3——4——5——6——7——8——9——10

YOUR PHYSICAL FITNESS: 1——2——3——4——5——6——7——8——9——10

WHAT YOU DO FOR FUN ON THE WEEKENDS: 1——2——3——4——5——6——7——8——9——10

THE PLACES YOU'VE VISITED IN THE WORLD: 1——2——3——4——5——6——7——8——9——10

THE AMOUNT OF MONEY YOU HAVE: 1——2——3——4——5——6——7——8——9——10

YOUR SENSE OF PURPOSE IN LIFE: 1——2——3——4——5——6——7——8——9——10

YOUR LIFE AS AN ADULT: 1——2——3——4——5——6——7——8——9——10

NOW GO BACK TO EACH OF THE ABOVE ITEMS AND PUT AN UP ARROW IF YOU THINK THINGS ARE IMPROVING OR A DOWN ARROW IF THINGS SEEM TO BE GETTING WORSE.

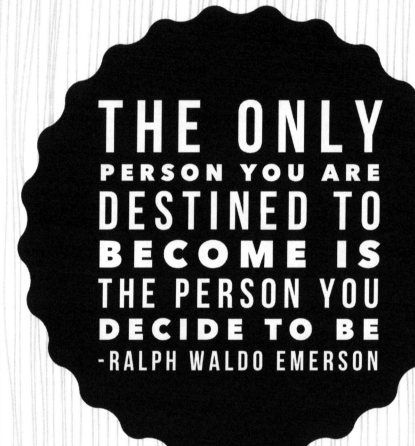

THE ONLY PERSON YOU ARE DESTINED TO BECOME IS THE PERSON YOU DECIDE TO BE
-RALPH WALDO EMERSON

IF YOU HAD TO TATTOO 5 WORDS ON YOUR ARM THAT EVERYONE WOULD SEE EVERY DAY FOR THE REST OF YOUR LIFE, WHAT WORDS WOULD YOU CHOOSE?

1.)

2.)

3.)

4.)

5.)

BONUS POINTS: DRAW AN IMAGE OR SYMBOL YOU WOULD TATTOO ON YOUR BODY.

THE REASON WE STRUGGLE **WITH INSECURITY** IS BECAUSE WE COMPARE OUR BEHIND-THE-SCENES WITH **EVERYONE ELSE'S** HIGHLIGHT REEL. -STEVEN FURTICK

DESCRIBE THE WORST THING THAT SOMEONE ELSE COULD SAY TO YOU.

NOW, DESCRIBE THE BEST THING THAT SOMEONE ELSE COULD SAY TO YOU.

BETTER TO WRITE
FOR YOURSELF
AND HAVE NO PUBLIC,
THAN TO WRITE
FOR THE
PUBLIC AND
HAVE NO SELF.
-CYRIL CONNOLLY

TAKE A MOMENT TO SKETCH YOUR DEEPEST FEAR BELOW:

BONUS POINTS: WHERE DO YOU THINK THIS FEAR MIGHT HAVE COME FROM? WHAT HAVE YOU DONE TO MINIMIZE THE CHANCE OF IT HAPPENING IN YOUR LIFE?

THE MUSIC IS NOT

in the notes, but in the

SILENCE BETWEEN.

-wolfgang amadeus mozart

WHAT IS AN ISSUE THAT YOU WISH PEOPLE WOULD TALK/CARE MORE ABOUT?

LIST 3 THINGS YOU COULD DO TO BRING MORE ATTENTION TO THIS CAUSE?

1.)

2.)

3.)

IF I CANNOT DO
GREAT THINGS,
I CAN DO
SMALL THINGS
IN A GREAT WAY
-MARTIN LUTHER KING JR

WHAT IS YOUR...

PROUDEST ACCOMPLISHMENT:

BIGGEST REGRET:

STRANGEST FEAR:

BIGGEST PET PEEVE:

TALENT NO ONE ELSE KNOWS ABOUT:

FAVORITE DRINK:

LEAST FAVORITE FOOD:

SECRET PASSION:

LEAST FAVORITE MUSIC GENRE:

FAVORITE TELEVISION SHOW GROWING UP:

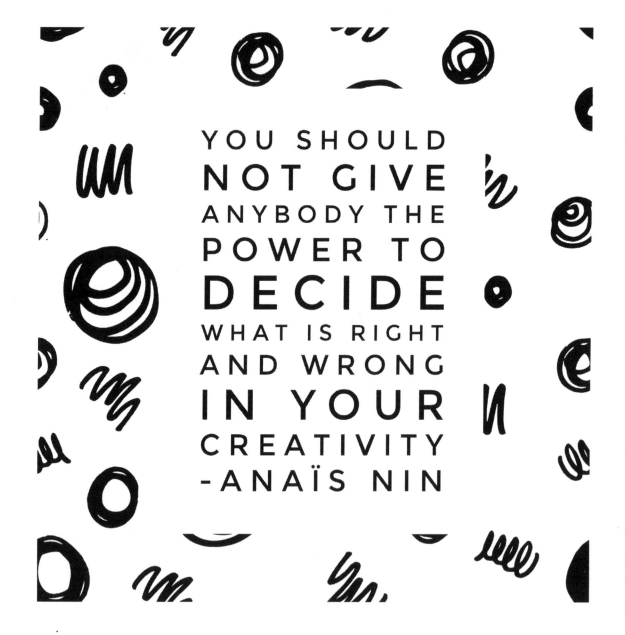

YOU SHOULD
NOT GIVE
ANYBODY THE
POWER TO
DECIDE
WHAT IS RIGHT
AND WRONG
IN YOUR
CREATIVITY
-ANAÏS NIN

DESCRIBE THE WORST PIECE OF ADVICE AN

KNOWING WHAT YOU KNOW NOW, WHAT WOULD YOU HAVE DONE DIFFERENTLY?

SELFISHNESS IS NOT LIVING AS ONE WISHES TO LIVE, IT IS ASKING OTHERS TO LIVE AS ONE WISHES TO LIVE.
-OSCAR WILDE

LIST 5 THINGS KIDS DO TODAY THAT YOU NEVER DID GROWING UP:

1.)

2.)

3.)

4.)

5.)

LIST 5 THINGS THAT YOU DID THAT YOUR KIDS NEVER WILL:

1.)

2.)

3.)

4.)

5.)

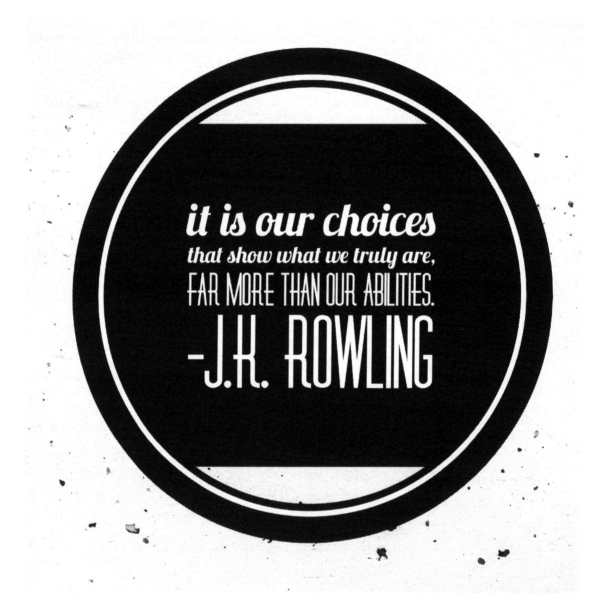

it is our choices
that show what we truly are,
FAR MORE THAN OUR ABILITIES.
-J.K. ROWLING

IF WE'RE BEING HONEST...

ON A SCALE OF 1-10, RATE YOUR PERSONALITY IN THE FOLLOWING AREAS

SELF-DISCIPLINE: 1—2—3—4—5—6—7—8—9—10

CURRENT LEVEL OF HAPPINESS: 1—2—3—4—5—6—7—8—9—10

LOYALTY TO OTHERS: 1—2—3—4—5—6—7—8—9—10

CREATIVE ABILITY: 1—2—3—4—5—6—7—8—9—10

LEVEL OF HONESTY: 1—2—3—4—5—6—7—8—9—10

PERSISTENCE: 1—2—3—4—5—6—7—8—9—10

PATIENCE: 1—2—3—4—5—6—7—8—9—10

INTELLIGENCE: 1—2—3—4—5—6—7—8—9—10

SENSE OF HUMOR: 1—2—3—4—5—6—7—8—9—10

GENEROSITY: 1—2—3—4—5—6—7—8—9—10

SELF-CONFIDENCE: 1—2—3—4—5—6—7—8—9—10

SPONTANEOUS: 1—2—3—4—5—6—7—8—9—10

FASHION SENSE: 1—2—3—4—5—6—7—8—9—10

SOCIALNESS: 1—2—3—4—5—6—7—8—9—10

HUMBLENESS: 1—2—3—4—5—6—7—8—9—10

OPTIMISM FOR THE FUTURE: 1—2—3—4—5—6—7—8—9—10

we know what we are,
BUT NOT WHAT
we may be.
-WILLIAM SHAKESPEARE

IF YOU WERE FORCED TO SING KARAOKE...

WHAT SONG WOULD YOU SING IF YOU WERE DRUNK?

WHAT SONG WOULD YOU SING IF YOU WERE SOBER?

WHAT SONG WOULD YOU SING AS A DUET?

WHAT SONG WOULD YOU SING AS PART OF A LARGE GROUP?

LOOKING AT THE STARS

ALWAYS MAKES ME DREAM.

-VINCENT VAN GOGH

WHEN IS THE LAST TIME YOU . . .

LAUGHED?

CRIED?

WERE AFRAID?

WERE ANGRY?

WERE IN LOVE?

WROTE A HANDWRITTEN LETTER?

FINISHED A NOVEL?

HUNG OUT WITH YOUR BEST FRIEND?

CALLED YOUR PARENTS?

READ A NEWSPAPER?

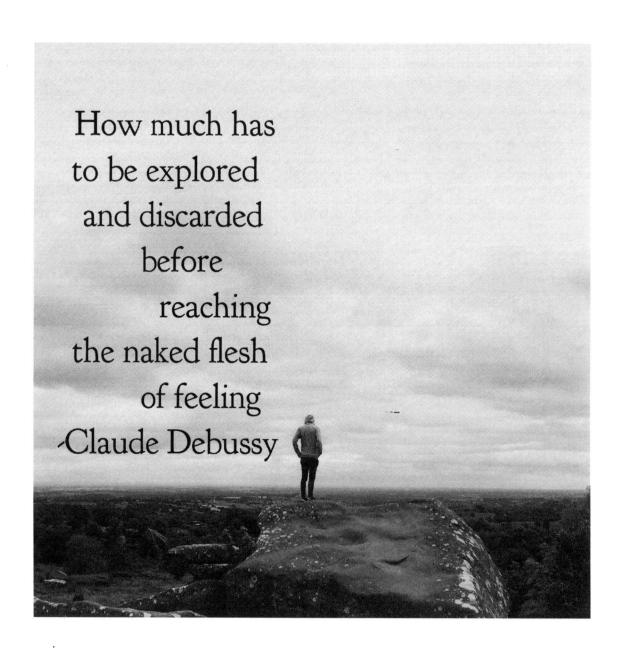

How much has
to be explored
and discarded
before
reaching
the naked flesh
of feeling
-Claude Debussy

WRITE DOWN 3 TITLES FOR YOUR FUTURE AUTOBIOGRAPHY:

1.)

2.)

3.)

WHICH ACTOR OR ACTRESS WILL PLAY YOU IN THE MOVIE?

WHO WILL PLAY THE OTHER LEADING ROLES?

IF YOU EVER FIND YOURSELF IN
THE WRONG STORY,
LEAVE.
-MO WILLEMS

WHAT WAS THE SMARTEST DECISION YOU MADE AS A TEENAGER?

WHAT WAS THE DUMBEST THING YOU DID AS A TEENAGER?

Keep away from
people who try
to belittle your ambitions.
Small people always do that,
but the really great
make you feel that you,
too, can become great
-Mark Twain

WHAT ARE 3 THINGS YOU WOULD LIKE TO CHANGE ABOUT YOURSELF THIS YEAR?

1.)

2.)

3.)

WHAT IS ONE THING ABOUT YOURSELF THAT YOU WOULD NEVER CHANGE?

ONLY THOSE
WHO WILL
RISK GOING
TOO FAR
CAN POSSIBLY
FIND OUT
HOW FAR ONE CAN GO
-T.S. ELIOT

WHAT WAS YOUR FAVORITE BOOK GROWING UP?

WHAT BOOK DO YOU WISH YOU WOULD HAVE READ SOONER?

WHAT BOOK DO YOU WISH YOU HADN'T READ AT ALL?

No need to hurry,
  no need to sparkle,
no need to be
        anyone but
        oneself
            -Virginia Woolf

LIST 3 THINGS THAT . . .

MOTIVATE YOU:

DISTRACT YOU:

COMFORT YOU:

MAKE YOU SAD:

MAKE YOU FEEL SAFE:

MAKE YOU WORRY:

YOU WANT TO LEARN MORE ABOUT:

MANY PEOPLE *lose* THE SMALL *joys in* THE HOPE *for the* BIG *happiness.*
-PEARL S. BUCK

DESCRIBE A TIME WHEN YOU FELT LIKE YOU MADE A DIFFERENCE IN SOMEONE'S LIFE.

NOW, DESCRIBE A TIME WHEN SOMEONE ELSE MADE A DIFFERENCE IN YOUR LIFE.

I KNEW WHO
I WAS
THIS MORNING,
BUT I'VE
CHANGED
A FEW TIMES
SINCE THEN
-LEWIS CARROLL

WHAT IS YOUR EARLIEST CHILDHOOD MEMORY? DESCRIBE IT IN AS MUCH DETAIL AS YOU CAN.

WHY DO YOU THINK THIS PARTICULAR MEMORY HAS STUCK WITH YOU OVER THE YEARS?

EXPECTING THE WORLD

TO TREAT YOU

FAIRLY BECAUSE

YOU ARE GOOD

IS LIKE EXPECTING

THE BULL NOT

TO CHARGE BECAUSE

YOU ARE A VEGETARIAN

-DENNIS WHOLEY

WHO ARE YOUR FAVORITE BANDS OR MUSICIANS RIGHT NOW?

1.)

2.)

3.)

4.)

5.)

WHO WERE YOUR FAVORITE BANDS OR ARTISTS GROWING UP?

1.)

2.)

3.)

4.)

5.)

TO PRACTICE
ANY ART,
NO MATTER HOW
WELL OR BADLY,
IS A WAY TO MAKE
YOUR SOUL GROW.
SO DO IT.
-KURT VONNEGUT

WHAT DID YOU WANT TO BE WHEN YOU WERE 10 YEARS OLD?

WHAT DID YOU WANT TO BE WHEN YOU WERE 20?

WHAT WOULD YOU LIKE TO BE DOING 10 YEARS FROM NOW?

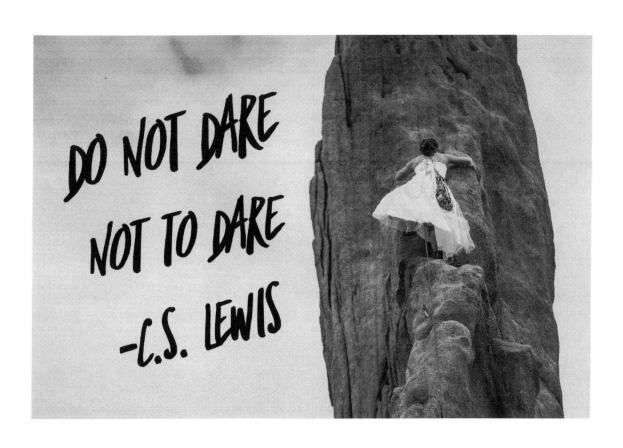

DO NOT DARE
NOT TO DARE

-C.S. LEWIS

DESCRIBE THE HARDEST CHOICE YOU EVER HAD TO MAKE.

DO YOU THINK YOU WOULD STILL MAKE THE SAME CHOICE TODAY?

IT'S BETTER TO FAIL IN ORIGINALITY, **THAN** SUCCEED IN IMITATION
-HERMAN MELVILLE

FINISH THE FOLLOWING SENTENCES:

I AM ALWAYS…

I AM NEVER…

I WANT MORE…

I WANT LESS…

I HAVE…

I HAVE NEVER…

I LOVE…

I HATE…

I WOULD LIKE TO BE BETTER AT…

I NO LONGER CARE ABOUT…

IN FIVE YEARS I WOULD LIKE TO…

FIVE YEARS AGO, I WISH I HAD…

WORDS ARE THINGS.
a small drop of ink,
FALLING LIKE DEW
upon a thought,
PRODUCES THAT WHICH
makes thousands,
PERHAPS MILLIONS, THINK.
- lord byron

IF YOUR LIFE WAS MADE INTO A MOVIE...

WHAT SONG WOULD PLAY DURING THE OPENING CREDITS?

WHAT SONG WOULD PLAY DURING THE ROMANTIC SCENES?

WHAT SONG WOULD PLAY DURING THE HAPPIEST PARTS?

WHAT SONG WOULD PLAY DURING YOUR LOWEST POINT?

WHAT SONG WOULD PLAY DURING THE CLOSING CREDITS?

YOU CAN'T STAY IN
YOUR CORNER
OF THE FOREST
WAITING FOR OTHERS
TO COME TO YOU.
YOU HAVE TO GO
TO THEM SOMETIMES
-A.A. MILNE

LIST ALL OF THE THINGS THAT YOU DIDN'T SAY OVER THE LAST MONTH BECAUSE YOU WERE AFRAID OF WHAT MIGHT HAPPEN.

DESCRIBE A TIME WHEN YOU DID SOMETHING EVEN THOUGH YOU WERE SCARED TO DO IT AT THE TIME.

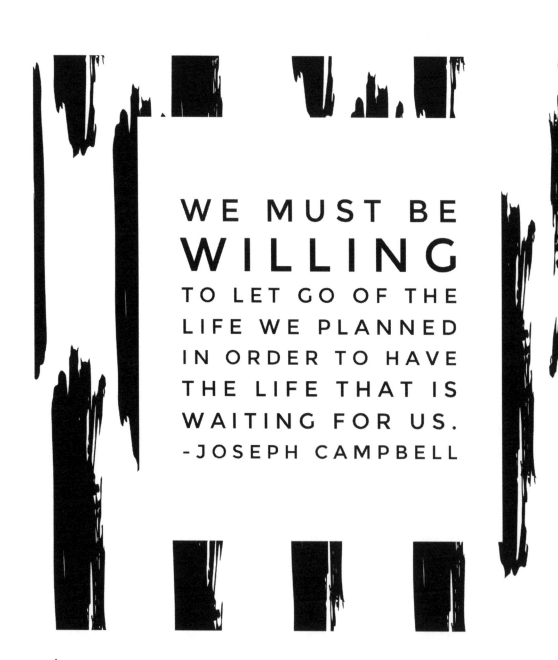

WE MUST BE
WILLING
TO LET GO OF THE
LIFE WE PLANNED
IN ORDER TO HAVE
THE LIFE THAT IS
WAITING FOR US.
-JOSEPH CAMPBELL

WHEN YOU ARE TALKING TO SOMEONE, WHAT ARE YOU MOST AFRAID THEY ARE GOING TO ASK YOU ABOUT?

HOW DO YOU USUALLY RESPOND WHEN THEY DO?

BONUS POINTS: WHY DO YOU THINK THIS SUBJECT BOTHERS YOU SO MUCH?

GO ON WORKING,
FREELY AND FURIOUSLY,
AND YOU WILL
MAKE PROGRESS.
-PAUL GAUGUIN

WHAT ARE 3 THINGS THAT YOU WISH SOMEONE HAD TOLD YOU TEN YEARS AGO?

1.)

2.)

3.)

BONUS POINTS: WHAT IS SOMETHING YOU WISH YOU HAD TOLD SOMEONE ELSE?

MANY MEN GO
FISHING ALL
OF THEIR LIVES WITHOUT
KNOWING THAT IT
IS NOT FISH
THEY ARE AFTER
-HENRY DAVID THOREAU

NAME YOUR TOP 5 FAVORITE CHARACTERS FROM A BOOK, MOVIE, OR TELEVISION SHOW:

1.)

2.)

3.)

4.)

5.)

BONUS POINTS: WHAT DO YOU ADMIRE MOST ABOUT THESE CHARACTERS? WHAT, IF ANYTHING, DO THEY HAVE IN COMMON?

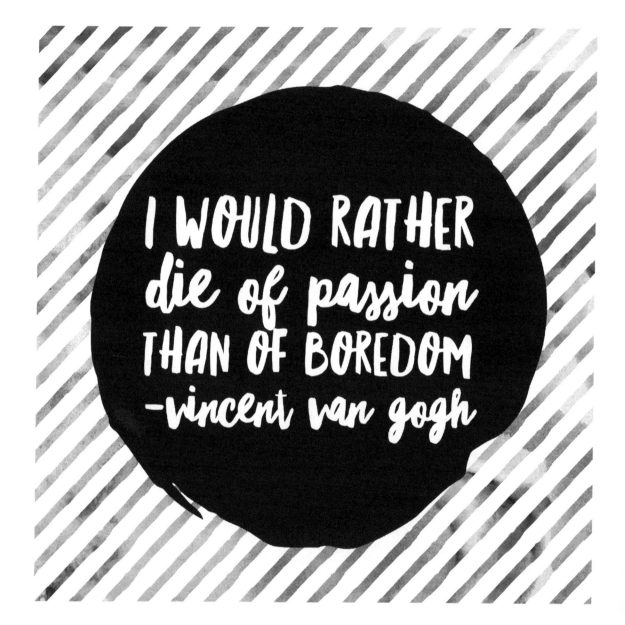

DESCRIBE YOUR PAST IN 3 WORDS:

1.)

2.)

3.)

DESCRIBE YOUR CURRENT LIFE IN 3 WORDS:

1.)

2.)

3.)

DESCRIBE YOUR FUTURE IN 3 WORDS:

1.)

2.)

3.)

my destination
IS NO LONGER A PLACE,
RATHER A NEW WAY OF SEEING.
-MARCEL PROUST

FILL OUT AS MANY OF THESE AS YOU CAN
(THE LESSONS YOU LEARNED CAN BE GOOD OR BAD)

THANKS TO _____ FOR TEACHING ME _____

THANKS TO _____ FOR TEACHING ME _____

THANKS TO _____ FOR TEACHING ME _____

THANKS TO _____ FOR TEACHING ME _____

THANKS TO _____ FOR TEACHING ME _____

THANKS TO _____ FOR TEACHING ME _____

THANKS TO _____ FOR TEACHING ME _____

THANKS TO _____ FOR TEACHING ME _____

THANKS TO _____ FOR TEACHING ME _____

If one only wished
          to be happy,
    this could be easily
               accomplished; but
            we wish to be happier
        than other people,
    and this is always
difficult, for we
believe others to be
        happier than they are
        -Montesquieu

WRITE DOWN FIVE OF YOUR FAVORITE THINGS YOU LIKE TO COOK:

1.)

2.)

3.)

4.)

5.)

IF YOU COULD PASS DOWN ONLY ONE OF THESE RECIPES TO YOUR FUTURE GRANDCHILDREN, WHICH ONE WOULD IT BE AND WHY?

BONUS POINTS: WRITE DOWN THIS RECIPE ON AN INDEX CARD AND THEN SEAL IT UP IN AN ENVELOPE. STICK THE ENVELOPE IN ONE OF YOUR COOKBOOKS WITH A NOTE.

START WHERE YOU ARE, USE WHAT YOU HAVE, DO WHAT YOU CAN

-ARTHUR ASHE

LIST ALL OF THE THINGS YOU WOULD LIKE TO ADD TO YOUR LIFE OVER THE NEXT YEAR:

NOW, LIST THE THINGS YOU WOULD LIKE TO SUBTRACT FROM YOUR LIFE OVER THE NEXT YEAR:

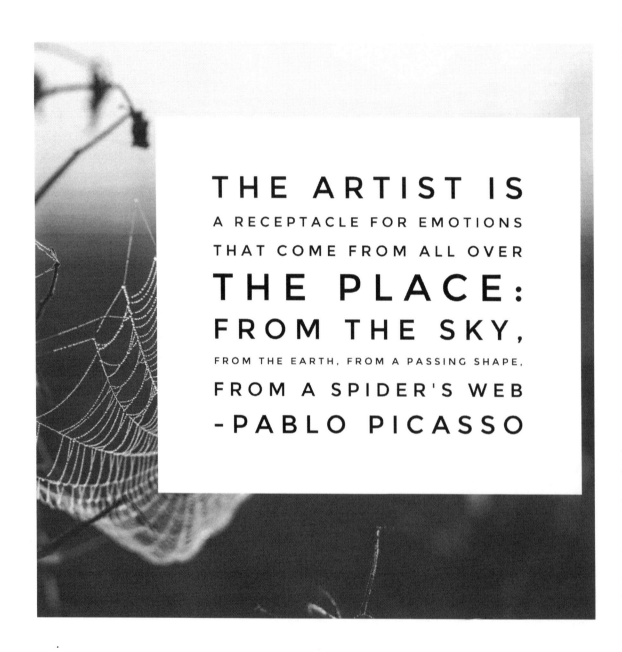

THE ARTIST IS
A RECEPTACLE FOR EMOTIONS
THAT COME FROM ALL OVER
THE PLACE:
FROM THE SKY,
FROM THE EARTH, FROM A PASSING SHAPE,
FROM A SPIDER'S WEB
-PABLO PICASSO

CREATE A FUN FACT ABOUT YOURSELF YOU WOULD BE WILLING TO TELL A STRANGER THAT ISN'T TRUE.

NOW COME UP WITH A SHORT BACKSTORY THAT EXPLAINS HOW IT ALL HAPPENED JUST IN CASE THEY ASK YOU FOR MORE DETAILS.

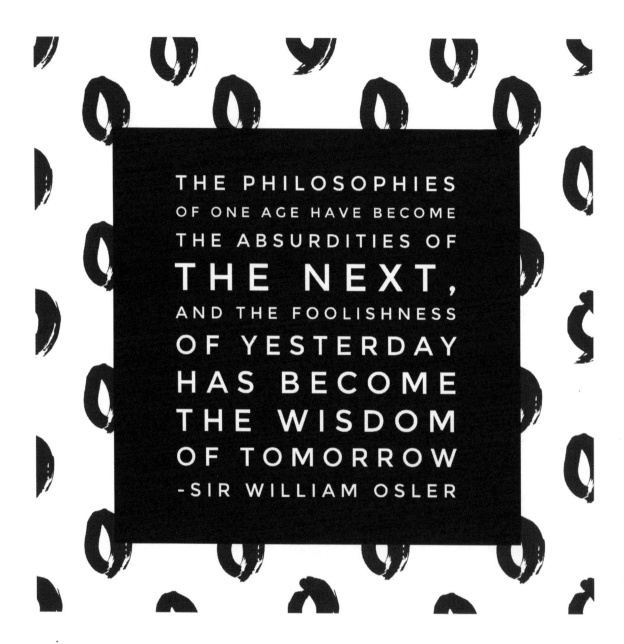

THE PHILOSOPHIES OF ONE AGE HAVE BECOME THE ABSURDITIES OF THE NEXT, AND THE FOOLISHNESS OF YESTERDAY HAS BECOME THE WISDOM OF TOMORROW
-SIR WILLIAM OSLER

QUAM BENE VIVAS REFERT NON QUAM DIU

(THE IMPORTANT THING ISN'T HOW LONG YOU LIVE, BUT HOW WELL YOU LIVE. ~SENECA)

COME UP WITH A PERSONAL MOTTO TO INSPIRE YOU OVER THE NEXT YEAR.

NOW TRANSLATE IT INTO A FOREIGN LANGUAGE SO THAT IT SOUNDS COOLER.

DON'T LET OTHER PEOPLE TELL YOU WHAT YOU WANT
- PAT RILEY

WHAT IS SOMETHING THAT YOU REGRET NOT TRYING TO DO WHEN YOU WERE YOUNGER
(MUSIC LESSONS, WRITING A BOOK, MOVING ACROSS THE COUNTRY, ETC...)

IS THIS SOMETHING THAT YOU WOULD STILL LIKE TO DO? IF SO, WHAT IS ONE THING YOU COULD DO TODAY TO MAKE IT HAPPEN?

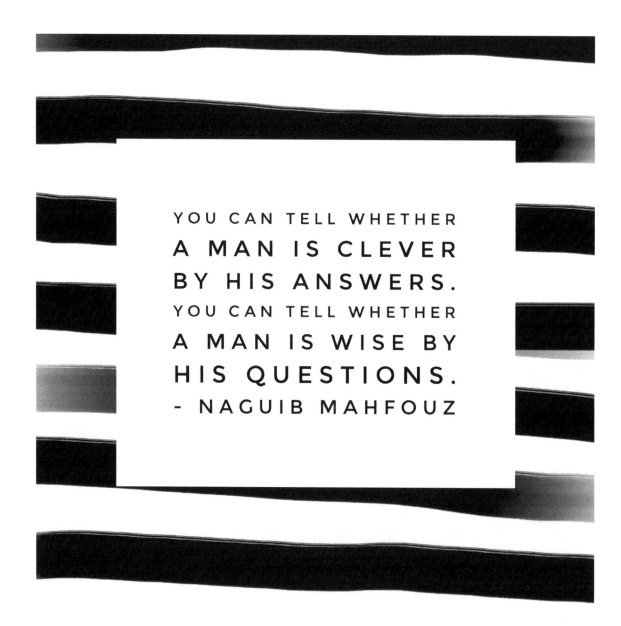

YOU CAN TELL WHETHER
A MAN IS CLEVER
BY HIS ANSWERS.
YOU CAN TELL WHETHER
A MAN IS WISE BY
HIS QUESTIONS.
- NAGUIB MAHFOUZ

HAVE YOU EVER HAD A COLLECTION OF SOMETHING?
(BOOKS, BEANIE BABIES, BEER CANS, POTATO CHIPS THAT LOOK LIKE CELEBRITIES, ETC...)

DESCRIBE YOUR COLLECTION:

HOW LONG DID YOU COLLECT THESE THINGS?

WHERE IS YOUR COLLECTION NOW?

BE SILLY, BE HONEST, BE KIND.
-RALPH WALDO EMERSON

IN TODAY'S DIGITAL WORLD, YOUR SIGNATURE IS ONE OF THE LAST HANDWRITTEN THINGS WE USE ON A DAILY BASIS.

TAKE A MOMENT AND SIGN YOUR NAME BELOW:

WHAT DO YOU LIKE AND NOT LIKE ABOUT YOUR SIGNATURE?

TRY WRITING YOUR SIGNATURE A FEW DIFFERENT WAYS AND SEE IF YOU LIKE IT BETTER:

P.S. IF YOU DECIDE TO CHANGE YOUR SIGNATURE, BE SURE TO NOTIFY YOUR BANK BEFORE YOU START BOUNCING CHECKS!

The question
isn't who
is going to let me,
it's who
is going to
stop me.
-Ayn Rand

CHOOSE FIVE ITEMS THAT ARE CURRENTLY IN YOUR HOUSE THAT WOULD BEST REPRESENT YOUR PERSONALITY TO FUTURE GENERATIONS IF YOU BURIED THEM IN A TIME CAPSULE:

1.)

2.)

3.)

4.)

5.)

WHAT ARE 2 THINGS IN YOUR HOUSE THAT YOU WOULD NEVER WANT ANYONE TO FIND IF SOMETHING HAPPENED TO YOU?

1.)

2.)

FAIL,
FAIL AGAIN,
FAIL BETTER.

• • •

Samuel Beckett

WHAT ARE 3 THINGS YOU THINK EVERYONE SHOULD EXPERIENCE AT LEAST ONCE IN THEIR LIFETIME?

1.)

2.)

3.)

P.S. HAVE YOU DONE ALL OF THESE THINGS YOURSELF?

TO DEFINE IS TO LIMIT.

-oscar wilde

IF YOU COULD WRITE ONLY ONE BOOK IN YOUR LIFE, WHAT TYPE OF BOOK WOULD IT BE AND WHAT WOULD IT BE ABOUT?

BONUS POINTS: SKETCH THE COVER OF YOUR BOOK BELOW

INSPIRATION COMES AND GOES, CREATIVITY IS

THE RESULT OF PRACTICE.

-PHIL COUSINEAU

NAME 3 PEOPLE YOU'VE NEVER MET WHO HAVE INFLUENCED YOU:

1.)

2.)

3.)

WHAT ARE THE THINGS THAT YOU ADMIRE MOST ABOUT THESE PEOPLE?

WHICH OF THEIR CHARACTER TRAITS ARE YOU CURRENTLY USING IN YOUR LIFE?

WHICH ONES ARE YOU STILL TRYING TO GET?

LEARN FROM YESTERDAY, LIVE FOR TODAY, LOOK TO TOMORROW, REST THIS AFTERNOON.
-CHARLES M. SCHULZ

WHAT ARE 10 THINGS YOU WOULD LIKE TO LEARN MORE ABOUT?

1.)

2.)

3.)

4.)

5.)

6.)

7.)

8.)

9.)

10.)

NOW PICK 2 OF THESE THAT YOU WILL START LEARNING ABOUT THIS MONTH.

1.)

2.)

THE ARTIST NEVER ENTIRELY KNOWS.
WE GUESS.
WE MAY BE WRONG,
BUT WE TAKE LEAP AFTER LEAP IN
THE DARK.
-AGNES DE MILLE

INVENT A NEW COLOR

GRAB SOME CRAYONS, PAINTS, OR COLORED PENCILS AND CREATE A BRAND NEW COLOR (OR AT LEAST A NEW SHADE OF ONE). ONCE YOU HAVE PERFECTED IT, COME UP WITH A CATCHY NAME FOR IT.

THE UNFED
MIND
DEVOURS
ITSELF.
-GORE VIDAL

DESCRIBE THE BEST THING THAT HAS HAPPENED TO YOU IN...

THE LAST WEEK:

THE LAST MONTH:

THE LAST YEAR:

THE LAST TEN YEARS:

SO FAR IN YOUR LIFETIME:

Never
put off
writing
until
you are
better at it.
-Gary Henderson

FIND AN OLD PHOTO FROM YOUR CHILDHOOD. DESCRIBE WHAT WAS GOING ON IN YOUR LIFE AT THAT TIME AND WHAT YOU WERE PROBABLY THINKING.

BONUS POINTS: CREATE A CAPTION FOR THIS PHOTO THAT SUMMARIZES YOUR LIFE AT THIS TIME.

LIFE IS
THE ART OF
DRAWING
WITHOUT
AN ERASER.
-JOHN W. GARDNER

WHAT ARE THE 3 WORST DECISIONS YOU HAVE EVER MADE?

1.)

2.)

3.)

WHAT ARE THE 3 BEST DECISIONS YOU HAVE EVER MADE?

1.)

2.)

3.)

AUTHOR'S NOTE

I just wanted to take a moment and say thanks again for picking up a copy of this writing journal. I know these days most of us are overwhelmed with choices that compete for our attention, so I really do appreciate you taking the time to go through it.

I hope that you found the prompts in this journal to be both inspiring and revealing. If so, I would simply ask you to consider leaving a review if you haven't already. It would really help me out as an independent author, and allow more people, just like you, to find this journal and perhaps discover something important about themselves along the way.

Thanks!

DREW ☺

I KNOW WHAT YOU'RE PROBABLY THINKING...

Wow, I just finished reading this awesome life-changing writing journal, which makes me wonder if this Drew character has written anything else that I might enjoy reading?

Well, you are in luck because it just so happens there are a few books out there available for your reading enjoyment. If you're interested, you can find out more about them below, or you can simply use the following link to visit my author page: **Author.to/DrewKimble**

Quiet Impact:
A Creative Introvert's Guide to the Art of Getting Noticed

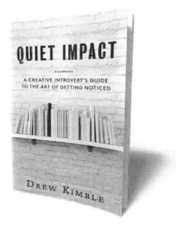

Are you an introvert trying to get noticed in a world full of noise? Learn how to take charge of your strengths and use them to your creative advantage.

Do you worry that being an introvert will hold you back in your creative endeavors? It's time to stop thinking that "being introverted" is a problem to be solved. This book will show you how to succeed by honing your natural abilities.

As the founder of SkinnyArtist.com, Drew Kimble has taught many introverts like you how to develop their creative strengths. By following his pragmatic advice, you'll learn how to get noticed in your field and share your story with your target audience, all the while never compromising who you are.

In *Quiet Impact*, you'll discover:

- Why being quiet isn't the same as being shy, weak, or unhappy
- How to minimize the toughest challenges of being an introvert
- The unspoken relationship rules for introverts and how to navigate them effectively
- How to market yourself without feeling like you're shouting
- How to thrive in a noisy, extroverted world, and much, much more!

The author knows from experience that you can get noticed without pretending to be something you aren't. Using a methodology that anyone can follow, you'll learn how to connect with your audience, show off your talents, and really take off in a world full of noise.

Quiet Impact is the creative manual for introverts who want to get noticed by all the right people. If you like practical guidebooks full of proven advice and plenty of "ah-ha!" moments, then you'll love Drew Kimble's career-changing book.

Buy *Quiet Impact* to connect with your audience the right way today!

Pick up your copy here: **myBook.to/QuietImpact**

Getting Creative:
Developing Creative Habits that Work

Plan. Fail. Repeat

How exactly does anyone have the time and energy to work on their creative projects after coming home from work, catching up on chores, and putting the kids to bed?

Do these people really have more time and energy than the rest of us, or were they were simply born with more self-discipline and motivation?

Maybe they stumbled upon some secret system that not only gives them the opportunity, but also the energy to create their art. Or maybe this is all just a bunch of crap that we tell ourselves in order to make us feel better.

Are you one of us?

If you are already a wildly successful writer, photographer, or visual artist who has more time than you know what to do with—this book probably isn't for you.

This book is for the rest of us who are frantically scurrying about our daily lives trying to juggle our kids, work schedule, and family responsibilities while still trying to find a few spare moments each day to do our creative thing.

Creativity isn't as easy as it looks

Unfortunately, creativity isn't some type of switch that you can simply turn on and off at random moments throughout the day. Sitting down to write isn't like throwing in a load of laundry or checking your email, where if you have a few spare minutes, you can still get something accomplished. In other words, you need to plan for creativity.

In *Getting Creative*, you'll discover:

- Why being motivated and having self-discipline isn't enough
- Understanding what habits can (and can't) do for you
- How to find and use your creative triggers
- Successfully managing your creative environment
- Why setting big goals for yourself is often a mistake
- How to hold yourself accountable without beating yourself up

Are you ready to get started?

Creativity is a habit like flossing your teeth—you either do it, or you just talk about doing it. Sure it would be great if we all had all the time and resources to do whatever we wanted to do, but that's rarely the way life operates, so we just have to do what we can with what we've got. Sometimes you just have to get creative to develop creative habits that work.

Pick up your copy here: **getBook.at/GettingCreative**

HANG OUT WITH US ONLINE

Writing long rambling books is only a small part of what I do. The rest of my time is spent writing long rambling blog posts, watching funny cat videos, yelling at small children (mostly my own), overfeeding our fat brown dog, and encouraging other creative souls to live their art.

If you would like to hang out, here's how we can connect:

Creative Ranting Website: **SkinnyArtist.com**
Publishing Website: **SkinnyCatStudios.com**
Facebook: **fb.com/LiveYourArt**
Twitter: **@SkinnyArtist**

About the author:

Drew is a writer, teacher, and head custodian of the Skinny Artist online creative community. He can often be found wandering about online, drinking lukewarm coffee, and avoiding any type of productive activity.

If you would like to share your thoughts, ask him a question, or simply say hello—he would love to hear from you. Take a minute and drop him a line at drew@skinnycatstudios.com

Legal mumbo-jumbo

Made in the USA
San Bernardino, CA
11 December 2018